# Kaleidoscope

Angie Ciarimboli

BookLeaf Publishing

India | USA | UK

Presentation by *BookLeaf Publishing*

Web: www.bookleafpub.com

E-mail: info@bookleafpub.com

ISBN: 9789360946616

First edition 2024

*To my soulmate and my best friend! Thank you for supporting me from beginning to end! I love you!*

# Kaleidoscope

Cosmos of colors
Fractured, yet still complete
Mosaic of life events
Shake. Kaleidoscope. Repeat.

Life is not linear
There are many hills and peaks
Minor disturbances
Shake. Kaleidoscope. Repeat.

Discovery of self
Personality diversity
New meaning to the meaning of life
Shake. Kaleidoscope. Repeat.

With creativity comes perspective
All tidy and neat
Change it up
Shake. Kaleidoscope. Repeat.

Decoupage of colors
Vibrant and complete
Patched together by circumstances
Shake. Kaleidoscope. Repeat.

Art in its many forms
Never obsolete
Bringing an attitude of change
Shake. Kaleidoscope. Repeat.

# Dandelion or Daffodil

Dandelion blowing in the wind
Spreading like wildfire
Bringing thoughts of all who've sinned
Spreading their poison, supplier.

Daffodil planted with care
Blooming in its glory
Swaying in the spring air
Telling the world its pampered story.

Dandelion or daffodil
Positive or plight
One survives due to sheer self-will
One has lived a life of delight.

Dandelion, a hearty perennial
Spawning with vigor
Life out of control
Experience of exile, trigger.

Daffodil, a beautiful flower
Smiling, oh so bright
Positive reinforcement, empower
Love at first sight.

Dandelion or daffodil
Positive or plight
One survives due to sheer self-will
One has lived a life of delight.

Dandelion situation
Seen as simply ugly weeds
Seeking validation
Judges by its misdeeds.

Daffodils delight
Assumed to be a precious blossom
Judged simply by sight
Seen, for their outward appearance only,
awesome.

Dandelion or daffodil
Positive or plight
One survives due to sheer self-will

One has lived a life of delight.

So, which one are you?
Dandelion or daffodil
Pampered life, do you pursue
Or do you survive by sheer will?

# Agitated

Agitated
Contemplative
Why does life have to be so hard?
Stressed out
Tapped out
Obsessed with change and I'm all out.

Illusions are the undreamt dreams;
Forcing their way through my imaginary reality.

Work hard
Play hard

Praying hard that it will all work out
When in doubt: scream and shout
Letting your voice be heard is what it's about.

Illusions are the undreamt dreams;
Fighting through this make-believe reality.

Day break
Hearts will ache
What will it take?
Mind, body and soul to partake.

Illusions are the undreamt dreams;
Seducing me thoroughly through my
make-believe reality.

Forsaken
Forgotten
Forging through the veil of time
Time stands still yet quickly rushes by.

Illusions are the undreamt dreams;
Scorching their way through my reality

Destruction
Despair
Lost to the evil in oneself; beware!
Tempting fate, my mistake
Allurement of the thing we fear.

Illusions are the undreamt dreams;
Becoming the heart of my reality.

The years
The fears
Push away at those too near
Mind clear
Sincere
Full steam ahead while steering clear.

Illusions are the undreamt dreams; closing the
gap.
Forever changing my trajectory.

# You versus me

You do you
I'll do me
Life goes on
You will see.

You do you
I'll do me
Two souls parting
Turbulent history.

You do you
I'll do me
Twin flame extinguished
Burned, 3rd degree.

You do you
I'll do me

Lies and accusations
Relationship debris.

You do you
I'll do me
Self-love and acceptance
Eventual recovery.

You do you
I'll do me
Life's too short
To live in misery.

You do you
I'll do me
Dream your dreams
Life expectancy.

# Wintertide

Snow crusted hills
Childhood thrills
Shouts and shrills
Winter time chills

Nostalgic feels
Sleigh ride peals
Kisses he steals
Laughter and squeals

Snowflakes falling
Children hollering
St. Nick holly jollying
Town square sprawling

Gifts and presents galore
Shopping at every store
Garland around every door
Christmas magic to explore

Music wafting through the air
Memories to make and share
Holiday merriment and cheer
Wintertide atmosphere

# Cavern of Fire

Cavern of fire
Flaming pyre
Relationship ire
What does this life require?

Smoldering ashes
Like poisonous gasses
Before your eyes, flashes
Life as it was, whiplashes.

Through the mire and muck
Feeling perpetually stuck
Positive experiences, new conduct
Poor life quality, reconstruct.

Never stationary, always improving
Negative actions and thoughts removing
New passion, all-consuming
New life path, blooming.

Freeing oneself through self-care
Noting past feelings of despair
Life is sometimes unfair
Looking ahead, prepare.

Becoming bailiwick down in your bones
Childish maneuvers outgrown
Negativity from others overthrown
Vibing in your own way, outshone.

So…

Cavern of fire
Elevating yourself higher
Exiting the mire
Doing what only you desire!

# What is Love

What is love?
Still trying to understand
The way we giggle while touching hands
The sweet surrender to well-made plans
What is love? The beauty of innocent friends.

What is love?
The yearning for another through the years
Memories, like unshed tears
Learning to live separately
Wondering what could be. Life is a journey.

What is love?
Your very essence sings to my soul
My happiness meter ticks out of control
I smile and laugh with playfulness and glee
At the thought of you reconnecting with me.

What is love?
I write mushy words and croon to love songs
My heart found what it was missing all along
Even if things never progressed as could be
You would remain the very best friend and first
love to me.

What is love?
With much anticipation I wait for our time
When I can hold you and make you mine
Changing my future one day at a time
Hoping you are my future and now you are
mine!

# Disengaged

Silence
Deafening, heartbreaking silence
Soulful words that never come
Leaving in its wake
The heart-breaking decision
To walk away.
I wasn't important enough to you
You obviously don't want me to stay
You're cold and disengaged
Causing questions, concerns, and rage
Do I stay?
Enraged at the thought
You chose other things
Over time with me
Plotting my response
How could I not matter to you?

After all our history
How could I leave?
But how?
How could I stay?
Say you want me
Tell me not to go
As my heart is shattered
My life, incomplete
Ghosted.
Silence
Deafening, heart-breaking silence
Soulful words that never come
Leaving in its wake
It is time to walk away.

# Unseen

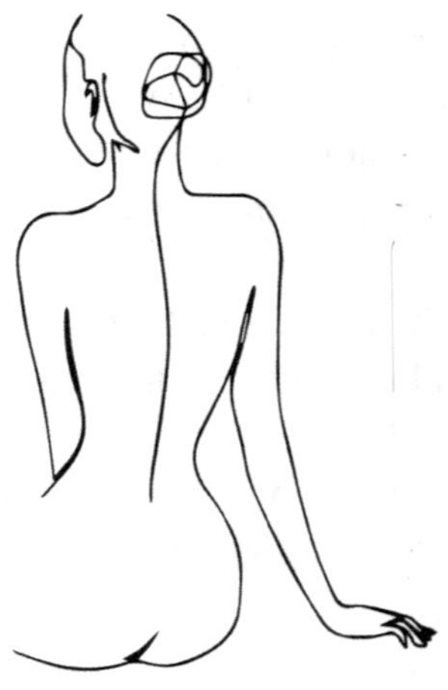

I punished myself cruelly
And froze up my pen
Until such a time was appropriate
When I picked it up again
I chewed up and swallowed my thoughts
My fears and my wounded heart
I was drowning in my silence
Making regret an art
Darkness swallowed me whole
But pretending to be strong
I convinced others I was "OK"
And kept on keeping on
But on the inside I was dying
My shattered heart: fragmented and dead

I could not confide in anyone
All thoughts of you kept locked away in my
head
Daily I suffered and died anew
Tormented emotions: Tears were shed
Whenever my thoughts would turn to you
It seems I was breathing: but at the same time,
still dead
Is this what it means to really love?
A question I have repeated to myself through the
years
I have searched and hunted for the answer
But I may have been missing something, I fear.

# Exit

I asked myself
Do I take what's mine
And walk away
With dignity in tact
It's too hard to stay
Situation out of my control
Too many unknowns
It hurts to go
But it hurts to stay.
And so, I think I'm done
Tired of the excuses
Making my exit
Heart and soul
No other way
To continue this life
No time spent
No tokens that you care
No artificial flowers

Nothing that reminds
Of the love we once shared
Wounded and tormented
By thoughts and questions
My heart split in two
Wondering what I should do
Should I walk the other direction
Throw in the towel
Or keep on trying
To make something out of nothing
Do I stay
Or do I set you free
To be all that you can be
Without me
To hold you back
Spreading your wings
While staying in check
Do I?

# The Sad Soul Of She

The weeping willows cry in painful mourning
Mother Earth cannot be consoled
One of her dear children has lost her way
Painting the world with the dark song of her
soul.
She wanders through the desolate valleys
Stained crimson with the blood of her tears
Roaming through the forgotten forests
In search of the light she hasn't seen in years.
Neither here nor there but rather wedged in
between
Always searching. There has got to be more to
life.
Never staying, never belonging
Spreads her wings in constant flight.
She wanders through the lush green hills
A moon child glowing with delight

An earthy wench of green and gold
Ever searching for the light.
She begs the universe for an awakening
Someone sent to earth who understands
The struggles and the trials
Of the girl who walks alone.
Trapped by society and its expectations
Who is eager to judge and to confirm?
Blessed with a higher consciousness of insight
To know, for her, there is no norm.
Misunderstood by many
Who ceases to comprehend?
Her heart it feels too much at times
Sometimes it only needs a friend.
Her instincts though they guide her
Often times leaving her alone
Where only the elect have tread
Through the deadly isolated zone.
The weeping willows cry in painful mourning
Mother Earth cannot be consoled
One of her dear children has lost her way
Leaving the world with the dark pain of her soul.

# Factual or Fantasy

Shades of green
Under the leafy canopy
Elves' unseen
Gathering.

Creatures of the woodland
Grazing on the hills
Little foresters' gathering nuts
Summertime thrills.

Woodland nymphs
Climbing cliffs

Mother, all-seeing
Hieroglyphs.

Butterflies in sunny meadows
Meandering flight
Summertime soiree
Excite.

Dandelions'
Wishes make
Magical world
Appreciate.

Slimy green frogs
Toadstool pedestal
Mushrooms for cover
Inedible.

Stealing apples from the orchard
Under the guise of night
Tricksters in the forest
Eating with delight.

Factual or fantasy
Only you can decide
In the eye of the beholder
Are they real, or do they hide?

# The Maze

There are days I struggle through the haze
As though I am the mouse and life is the maze.

Something different around every bend
Wondering if the tribulation will ever come to an
end.

Through the seasons of life, sometimes
undetected
Twists and turns and situations unexpected.

Problems and trials once concealed
Anxiety and stress do readily yield.

Twists and turns and dead ends
Forward, backwards, transcends.

Through the gamete of life day by day
Pushing through to make a way.

Forward through the muck and mire
Making a way ahead as I desire.

There are days I struggle through the haze
As though I am the mouse and life is the maze.

# Fool for You

Time and space may barrier be
When distance separates us
And karma displaces us
From each other's arms where we long to be.

Only fools fall in love they say
Then I'll be a fool for you any day.

My mind is warped on thoughts of you
My heart flutters and sings
My tummy does funny flipflop things
I close my eyes and dream of you.

Only fools fall in love they say
Then I'll be a fool for you any day.

I hope that this separation
Is a way for preparing?
At you, the way I be staring
Of free will and not obligation.

Only fools fall in love they say
Then I'll be a fool for you any day.

Every day and night I'm scheming
Hoping to connect in this life
With the man who looks like sin
To see if our love's worth is seeming.

# The Flame

Flame flickers
Wax burns
Feelings dwindle
Heart yearns.

Flame flickers
Wax burns
Time extinguished
Tide turns.

Flame flickers
Wax burns
Affections disintegrate
Motives observed.

Flame flickers
Wax burns
Elongated connection
Friends with perks.

Flame flickers
Wax burns
Only thinking of self
Self-serve.

Flame flickers
Wax burns
Moving up and moving on
Quality deserved.

Flame flickers
Wax burns
Lovers and players
Two wordy nerds.

Flame flickers
Wax burns
One and done
Call the hearse.

Flame flickers
Wax burns
Goodbye my friend
Love hurts!

# Hopeless

Hopeless
Pit of despair
Helpless
Because you aren't there.

Lonely
Entombed in my thoughts
Autopilot
Seemingly controlled by bots.

Desolate
Failure to thrive
Breathing but living?
Dead or alive.

Wanting but wasting
Away, day by day

Dreaming of escaping
Determined to find a way.


Discouraged
Drudgery in the way
Seeking to be encouraged
Hoping you would stay.

Clouded distant dreams
Fairy tales in reality
Never finding what I seek
That is my eternal fallacy.

Dehydration
Water station not found
Escalation
Pulling me towards the ground.

Retribution
Seeking of the inner peace
Execution
Hanging from the guillotine.

# Taste of Night

Breathtaking in the night sky is the glorious
moon
Who lets us know when we wake whether it's
too soon
Jumped over in the tales by the fork and the
spoon
Whose fragrant sight lingers like expensive
perfume.

The stars how they sparkle like tiny bright
jewels
Each one has a story, each is a tool

Burning ever bright seemingly never to cool
Until the sun comes up and the children go to
school.

The crackling of logs with orange iridescent
glow
The hum of the flame as they lick at the bows
Sending forth their spark to again never know
Until it is winter and the campfire goes.

Tastes of night for blessed child
Sometimes torrid and at other times mild
Advocate for nature's fury wild
Oh, sacred night how you have beguiled.

# Incisions

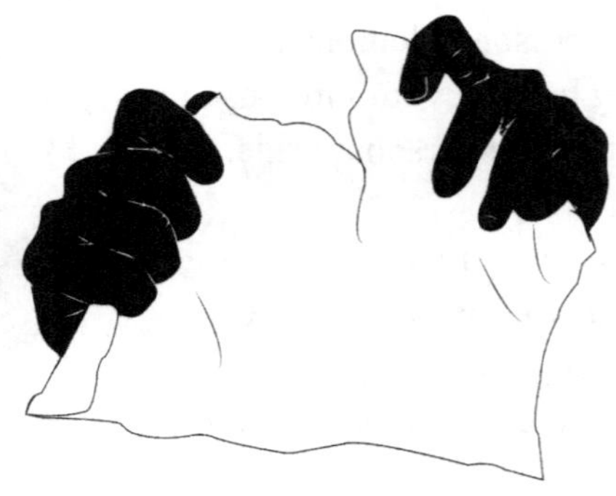

Incisions
Rising up out of the skin
Decisions
Knowing just where to begin.

What do they share in common?
Nothing it would seem
But take a closer look
And you will see what I mean.

Incisions like decisions
Cutting the excess away
Getting down to the basics
By leaving or deciding to stay.

Both scenarios require a choice
And a willingness to identify
Those toxic traits in your own life

Not just casting the blame, outcry.

Putting off the pride of self
Casting personal demons aside
Moving beyond your circumstances
Growing with personal pride.

Today is not forever
The pain will one day subside
If you keep on moving forward
Through the tears that you have cried

So, keep on moving and growing
Working on me, myself and I
For all the effort you put into it.
Will someday multiply?

And then one day you will turn the corner
Your happiness will bloom
You will rediscover who you were again
And only positive things will have room.

So, keep on keeping on
I know the pain of today is rough
Take things one day at a time
You are freaking tough!

# Suffering Alone

Dying on the inside
Heart about to explode
Shards of shattered glass
Penetrating the essential organ
Agony
Insurmountable pain
Dark times
Dark thoughts
Purpose no more
Lost to suffering
Suffering alone.

# Lavender Fields

Lavender fields
Serenity yields
No more armor and shield
Old wounds healed.

Petals of peace
Sweet release
Dreams never cease
Rain drops obese.

Bubble baths and sleep
Secrets to keep
Sprouts of purple, deep
Aromas do seep.

Dreams abound
Wishes found
Waterfalls crowned
At the alluring sound.

# Statement of Void

Annoyed
Played and toyed
Trust destroyed
Relationship void.

Broken
Harsh words spoken
No love token
Mistrust awoken.

Distressed
Emotions suppressed
Highly stressed
Progress regressed

Drama

Too many baby momma
Starting over, gonna
Chew you up, piranha.

Nice?
Think twice
Is it worth the price?
Sacrifice.